TABLE OF CONTENTS

BRIEF HISTORY OF YOGA	1
DEFINITION OF YOGA	3
BENEFITS OF YOGA	5
YOGA HEALTH BENEFITS	7
THE MAIN TYPES OF YOGA	13
YOGA FOR BEGINNERS: TIPS FOR GETTING STARTED	23
HOW YOGA SESSION TIPS WORK	28
YOGA BEGINNERS STYLES	30
HOW TO CHOOSE YOUR STYLE?	35
YOGA POSITION/POSTURE FOR BEGINNER	42
GENTLE POSES FOR RELAXATION AND HEALING	53
YOGA: HEALING THROUGH ASANAS	58
DIFFERENT WAYS TO REACH SAME DESTINATION IN YOGA	67
THE ADVANTAGES OF YOGA IN LIFE AS A COUPLE	111
COMPLEMENTARY, INTEGRATIVE, AND ALTERNATIVE HEALTH APPROACHES	113
CONCLUSION	118

BRIEF HISTORY OF YOGA

The word Yoga comes from the Sanskrit root "Yuj" Which means **Union.** Through this union, the individual can then experience the union of the **individual consciousness** with **the universal one.** Yoga has evolved to become one of the most commonly practiced practices in the world. Today it is recognized as a "curative" or at least complementary practice in the treatment of many pathologies and conditions. National Health Interview Survey (NHIS) reports that the most common reasons adults and children engage in yoga are for relieving chronic lower back pain, improving general health, reducing stress, and improving fitness, overall strength and flexibility especially in relation to physical exercise (even at a competitive level).

Yoga is believed to be over 5000 years old, according to information from the oldest texts of mankind, the Vedas.

The practice of Yoga and its culture was passed from teacher to disciple verbally, it was said that it was from word of mouth, later they began to be transcribed which still stands till date. There are still some practices that can only be accessed through the great teachers found in India, but it is very difficult to reach them.

Today we have at our disposal innumerable information such as books, videos, magazines and this makes Yoga accessible to a lot of people.

DEFINITION OF YOGA

Yoga is the practice of a set of postures and breathing exercises aimed at providing physical and mental well-being which denotes a precise and sophisticated knowledge of physiological processes, as well as psychic processes and the interaction and mutual influence between mind and body.

It is a complex and immense theoretical-practical corpus that includes a philosophy, a cosmogony, a refined psychology, a mysticism, a detailed study of the states of consciousness together with the means and conditions to achieve them, an evolutionary spiritual process without necessarily being linked to any specific religion. Yoga is also a science of psycho-physical well-being.

BENEFITS OF YOGA

Approaching yoga for beginners is a first step to embark on a great journey of self-discovery.

The benefits of yoga are visible in both the short and long term.

Stress Reliever: Practicing yoga regularly is good for stress. There are many yoga exercises against anxiety and stress, useful for relaxing and letting go of worries;

Improvement of brain functions: According to an American study, following a 20-minute practice of Hatha Yoga, an improvement in cognitive functions and an increase in attention and memory at work can be found. This makes yoga even more suitable for regaining your concentration for study;

Improved Flexibility: Some **yoga** poses help improve flexibility in the legs, shoulders, and back.

Helps to keep Body weight under control: According to some studies, practicing yoga regularly helps to keep body weight under control and also to burn calories. Yoga and exercises to lose weight, therefore, are by no means an unlikely combination.

Moderates Blood Pressure: Some research has shown that people with mild or moderate hypertension could derive multiple benefits from Yoga, which would help lower blood pressure.

Habits of Life: yoga for beginners helps to acquire new habits and a healthier lifestyle, which also takes into account the right diet.

As in meditation , by listening to your breathing and listening to your sensations, yoga promotes letting go by living in the present moment.

You will forget everyday worries and automatic thoughts.

After a yoga session, you will feel relaxed and you will have regained energy.

YOGA HEALTH BENEFITS

The general benefits of yoga have been discussed previously, in this section the health benefits of yoga according to science will be discussed.

Lowers anxiety and control's stress

Practicing yoga regularly (especially when combined with other stress relievers like walking outdoors or meditation) can help combat many physical manifestations of stress and anxiety. This is due to the benefits that yoga brings to the central nervous system (CNS) and the immune system.

Research conducted by the Institute for Behavioral Medicine Research at Ohio State University found that yoga minimizes secondary inflammatory responses to

stressful events. After comparing 25 yoga beginners to 25 yoga experts, the researchers found that regular yoga sessions have:

- Enhanced control of participants on inflammatory or endocrine responses;

- Lowered serum interleukin (IL) levels by as much as 6 times;

- Reduced levels of C-reactive protein (CRP);

- Caused decreased stimulation of lip polysaccharides in response to stressful events.

Improved quality of Sleep

Yoga is one of the natural remedies for poor sleep related issues. Studies show that 4 to 8 weeks of yoga is enough to have a positive effect on the quality and even quantity of sleep, even in people who have a real insomnia disorder.

For many, lack of night's sleep is the result of high levels of stress, hormonal imbalances or chronic pain and particular conditions. Taking regular time to "tune into your body" can teach you to recognize the first warning signs it sends when you are in a state of suffering or even just about to feel pain and then take action to prevent the stress response from manifesting itself. With worse effects, such as the aforementioned; difficulty in falling asleep and staying asleep. Since yoga helps activate the **parasympathetic nervous system** (PNS) and decreases **sympathetic nervous system** (SNS) activity, it can reduce sleep disturbances and help treat symptoms of insomnia.

It improves the flexibility and range of joint movements

The International Journal of Yoga showed that regular yoga practice can increase athletes' flexibility, balance, and even performance. After 10 weeks of practice, flexibility and balance measurements improved in tests to measure these specific parameters. Yoga is also one of the practices to improve the functioning of the psoas (or iliopsoas) muscle, an abdominal muscle core that lies deep and is called the "muscle of the soul". A healthy psoas muscle is linked not only to improve movement but also to better emotional health.

Helps to improve balance and prevent falls

Maintaining balance is a real panacea for the elderly. It helps them stay healthy and maintain independence in their movements. While younger people may take balance as a present element of their body image for granted, it is vitally important for the elderly and those who are losing this all-important self-perception over the years.

Reduces fatigue and "brain fog", a particular condition present in diseases such as Chronic Fatigue Syndrome (or CFS)

When our circadian rhythm is perfect and functions regularly, with the right sleep-wake cycles, it will be difficult to experience this sort of mental confusion (of a different entity) which is commonly identified as "brain fog". An inexplicable fatigue and lack of concentration at other times can cause problems at work and in everyday relationships, favoring adaptation processes that do not always go hand in hand with the success of a peaceful and pleasant life.

Yoga is often considered an effective way to increase focus and energy, both for the body and mind. The stretching itself, even for short periods of 1 or 2 minutes, can produce enormous effects on energy levels, especially for people who spend long hours sitting at a desk and staring at the screen of a computer.

Yoga exercises that help you feel more awake and alert include: bending and touching your toes (forward bend), alternating squatting and then standing with your hands above your head, any form of backward bend or even a short 10-minute break to practice a breathing or meditation exercise.

It could help reduce pain

Studies show that certain yoga poses can help reduce lower back pain, neck pain, and migraines. In addition to this, the benefits of yoga also include improving the ability to walk and move, managing symptoms of arthritis, and improving digestive disorders.

The improved flexibility and blood flow not only help to control pain, but the yoga practice itself, helps the individual mentally to experience pain differently and learn to manage it in the right way. The essence of this improvement lies precisely in the contribution that this discipline gives to the brain by transforming the body into a sort of "pain reliever of itself".

It can help stimulate weight loss and fortify muscles

Sometimes you may ask yourself: does yoga count as a valid exercise for muscle hypertrophy, is it a fitness practice? The quick answer is no. This is of course true when considering the recommended 30 minutes of moderate physical activity each day.

Some yoga styles that are more intense and protracted for longer periods of time, both in the single session and in the entire course, can help promote weight loss (or the maintenance of a healthy weight) by reducing inflammation, balancing hormones, controlling appetite, increasing muscle mass and promoting metabolism. Although some yoga classes can definitely make you sweat, burn a lot of calories, and tone your entire body.

It can be said with certainty that most of the benefits derived from yoga can be considered as transversal, deriving from a series of perceptual modifications that yoga uses on our body and mind, because trust in one's body, believing that having the ability to heal or change, are emphasized by yoga. Many studies have found that yoga can help overcome various insecurities related to one's body: eating disorders, digestive disorders that affect appetite or wrong food choices, resulting in a virtuous circle of self-improvement that will undoubtedly lead to a better quality of life and an overall improvement of one's image.

THE MAIN TYPES OF YOGA

1. Ashtanga yoga
2. Bikram yoga
3. Hatha yoga
4. Iyengar yoga
5. Jivamukti yoga
6. Kripalu yoga
7. Kundalini yoga
8. Power yoga
9. Sivananda
10. Viniyoga
11. Yinyoga
12. Yoga Nidra
13. Hot Yoga
14. Prenatal Yoga

15. Restorative Yoga

Yoga is a discipline that comes in 20 different approaches and hundreds of postures called "ASANAS". I will explain in a few words what are the main yogas practiced.

Ashtanga Yoga

This system is based on six sequential series of asanas that increase in difficulty. Before moving on to the next series, it is essential to have a perfect mastery of the series. In class, the series are linked quickly, and the postures are Coordinated with a particular breathing pattern (Ujjayi). The series are fixed and never change. Be prepared to sweat. Ashtanga Yoga is a vigorous style of yoga that requires good physical condition, suitable for young people, athletes and those seeking intense physical activity.

Bikram

This yoga is practiced in a humid room heated to 40 °, sauna-type effect. Sweat helps flush toxins out of the body. The heat promotes flexibility and weight loss. The rooms are often full, a shower is necessary at the end of the session. Its founder Bikram Choudhury has sequenced a series of 26 traditional hatha postures that are always the same in each class. It is reserved for people in excellent physical condition and not recommended for people with heart disease.

Yoga Nidra

This type of yoga will allow you to let go and relax deeply. It is ideal for combating stress. Its asanas are based on concentration and breathing.

Hot yoga or Bikram yoga

It's the yoga for everyone: novices or experts. This involves twenty-six postures and two breathing exercises that allows you to work on stretching and breathing. Hot yoga is practiced in a room heated to 40 ° and for 90 minutes to promote the elimination of toxins.

The Iyengar

This practice is the most demanding, because it works the perfect alignment of the body. Reserved for experienced practitioners, iyengar is broken down into sequences and 23 basic postures. It is very demanding and requires intensive practice. When your body is more flexible, you gain confidence, balance and vitality.

Hatha Yoga

It is the most practiced yoga in the West. The word "Ha-Tha" symbolically means the union of the moon and the sun, of opposing energies, of duality. It is a physical discipline that mainly focuses on postures and the breath to purify the body and provide the physical strength necessary for long meditations. Typically, classes consist of yoga postures, breathing exercises, and finally relaxation. Concentration and meditation techniques can be part of the course. Yoga sessions vary according to the teacher; the sequences are rather slow apart from the sun salutation and the static postures, maintained for quite a long time. Hatha yoga is suitable for everyone, and at all levels with learning at their own pace, more advanced postures. It is a fairly gentle, non-competitive practice that aims at maintaining good vitality and health at all ages. Perfect for beginners, it allows you to assimilate the postures and learn to link breathing to movement, which are the basics of yoga . Hatha yoga is for those who want to be calmer, eliminate stress, improve flexibility and regain their energy.

Sivananda (Global, Spiritual)

Among the schools of Hatha yoga, Swami **Sivananda** (swami means monk), is the best known. It is a physician from Rishikesh, India, who taught his disciples to "serve, love, give, purify, meditate, realize". **Vishnudevananda** presented these teachings to a Western audience and founded the international centers of Sivananda Yoga Vedanta. Hatha yoga practice emphasizes the sun salutation and 12 basic postures to increase the strength and flexibility of the spine. Chanting, pranayama, and meditation are also included. Sivananda Yoga is for those for whom the philosophical and spiritual aspect is important. Another famous disciple of Sivananda, **Swami Satyananda**, also popularized yoga in the West and created the Bihar School of Yoga which has published many reference yoga books. Hatha yoga practices are inspired by tantra yoga. It was Swami Satyananda who developed **Yoga Nidra**. This deep relaxation technique is based on breathing and visualization exercises that facilitate a state of deep letting go and touching the spheres of the subconscious. It improves sleep, self-awareness and brings a more serene mind. Sophrology is also inspired by it.

Vinyasa Yoga

A very popular type of yoga in the West, Vinyasa, sometimes called flow yoga, is a softer, freer and more accessible version of traditional Ashtanga yoga. It is a dynamic sequence where the positions are linked in a fluid way to the rhythm of the breath. This practice is quite physical, it is better suited to people with an intermediate level and who are looking for a tonic and creative yoga.

Yoga Iyengar

The great master Iyengar was a pupil of Krishnamacharya during his youth. Iyengar yoga emphasizes placement, body alignment and precision in postures. The poses are held for a while. The specificity and creativity of Iyengar is the use of accessories, like straps, chairs, blocks and blankets, to suit beginners and those with little flexibility. Accessories can also meet special needs such as injuries or structural imbalances. It is accessible to all, by levels (from beginners to experienced), it is suitable for perfectionists and those who like strict teachers on the precision of postures. Derived from Iyengar, Restorative Yoga is more relaxing, the postures are held for a long time up to 20 minutes.

Yin yoga (passive and meditative)

Inspired by Chinese medicine, Yin yoga is a slow yoga where postures are held for nearly 5 minutes to stretch the connective tissues (ligaments, tendons) and activate the energy meridians in the body. By means of blankets, bricks, duffel bags, the practitioner settles "comfortably" in the posture. The challenge is to stay still in the posture. Yin yoga aims to cultivate inner silence and letting go, inviting moments of meditation. It is a great addition to other more active forms of yoga, such as Vinyasa, for deep relaxation. It is accessible to everyone, but requires mental strength and patience.

Power Yoga

Power Yoga was developed in the United States from Yoga Asthanga in order to make it more accessible to Western students while maintaining physical intensity. The sequences are not fixed and the courses vary. The popularity of Power Yoga has spread to fitness clubs; it is suitable for sportsmen and athletes.

Unlike Vinyasa, Power yoga postures are held longer and seek muscle strengthening. There is less attention to breathing and fluid movements like in Vinyasa. Not to be confused with **Hot**

Power Yoga which is practiced in rooms heated to 30° in the spirit of Bikram Yoga, where the sequences are however not fixed, of the Vinyasa type.

Kundalini Yoga

Derived from tantra, it has long remained a closely watched secret and practiced only by a few. In 1969, Yogi Bhajan decided to change this tradition by bringing Kundalini yoga to the West. The Kundalini designates a primordial energy located at the base of the spine. Practitioners focus on awakening energy, seeking to raise it upward through the seven chakras, master it, and thus raise one's consciousness and harness its potential. The session is composed of dynamic postures at a sustained pace, breathing techniques, mantra recitations, chants and meditations. This yoga is suitable for students in good physical condition.

Ananda Yoga (energetic, spiritual)

It is a classic gentle Hatha yoga developed by Swami Kriyananda in the USA in the 1960s. Swami Kriyananda trained with Master Paramhansa Yogananda, author of the famous book *Autobiography of a Yogi*. One of its specificity is to maintain the postures by repeating silent affirmations. Classes also focus on alignment, and controlled breathing exercises to promote self-awareness. Ananda yoga is suitable for those who aspire to higher goals of spiritual growth while releasing tension from the body.

Kriya Yoga (practical, spiritual)

Kriya Yoga was revived by the great master Babaji in India. This form of yoga represents a synthesis of traditional teachings. It includes a set of 144 Kriyas or "cleanses", grouped into 5 phases or categories. It brings together the bodily or energetic techniques of Hatha yoga, Kundalini yoga, and Tantra yoga.

The emphasis is on practice, effort, perseverance and work on oneself. The goal being the union of the being with the Absolute Reality by the realization of the Self. Today yoga classes mainly offer physical exercises and some breathing practices. They are relieved of the meditative and more spiritual aspect of the traditional ways. Before becoming westernized, yoga in India was based on four traditional paths of yoga (called marga) that lead to self-realization and liberation:

- **Bhakti yoga**, or the yoga of devotion, it is based on chanting and devotion, it's most popular in India

- **Karma yoga**, or yoga of selfless action and service, it is based on the writings of the *Bhagavad-Gita*

- **Jnana yoga**, or yoga of knowledge, it goes through introspection and discrimination (reserved for advanced practitioners)

- **Raja yoga**, or royal yoga, the most complete, it is based on the eight principles (ashtanga) of Patanjali. It includes the 3 previous yoga (Bhakti, Karma and Jnana) and Hatha yoga. Depending on your need, you will orient yourself towards one or another form of yoga, whether traditional or modern, knowing that hatha yoga is the most common form in the West.

YOGA FOR BEGINNERS: TIPS FOR GETTING STARTED

1. Focus on your motivations.

Especially in big cities you will find a wide offer of yoga classes: from the most relaxing Yin Yoga to the spirit-centered Kundalini, to the most intense sessions of Power Yoga. Ask yourself why you want to start practicing yoga and what aspects do you think are important in a beginner class or in a school. At this point, look for the yoga centers that meet your criteria and choose the style in line with your goals.

2. Find a yoga center

If you are still starting out, it is good to go to a yoga school, especially if you are a complete beginner. Practicing yoga in a group is more fun and while following the instructions of a qualified teacher you will perform the sequences most suitable for the level of the class. And if you make any incorrect movements, the instructor will provide you with the necessary help and will show you the possible variations in case any position is difficult for you.

3. Discover the wheel that's right for you

Sometimes yoga is enjoyable from the very first lessons, but sometimes it doesn't. Obviously the better you can do something, the more fun it is. If the first attempts are not an immediate success, don't be discouraged, but give yourself time to familiarize yourself with the exercises and learn the routines of the lessons. To understand if the school, the teacher and the style are right for you, it would be good to follow the course for a month, attending 2 or 3 times a week. If that's not your thing, then look elsewhere.

4. Be realistic

Upright or lotus postures are impressive postures, but they are not suitable for beginners. After all, you can't get up one morning and sign up for a marathon just because you always wanted to. The risk of not completing it is high, not to mention that of getting hurt. **Ask the yoga center what level is right for you** and stick to the advice they give you.

5. No comparison with others

Easy to say, yet it is not. Think about it for a moment: if you are a beginner, what sense does it make to compare your level with that of those who have practiced the discipline for years? And why should being able to do splits make you feel better than other beginners when you know you've been taking dance lessons for years? Focus on yourself and keep your past experiences in mind. Just like in any sport, everyone's body reacts differently. And it is so beautiful!

6. Better not to overdo it

The first few times you practice yoga, move calmly and slowly. It is not really the case to overdo it, nor to want everything immediately. Every now and then try to ask yourself if everything is okay. Are the joints in the right positions? Do you feel any pain? Do you think this position is suitable for you? If the answer is yes, then you can go a little further and practice the asana deeper and deeper. Before yoga it is also important not to overdo the food: by the time you unroll the mat it should have been about 3 hours since your last full meal. Instead, drink some warm water, which is good for the stomach and refreshes the spirit. Water is fine, but with tea there is more taste.

7. There is no rush

Do you have all the credentials to dedicate yourself to strength training or a walk? Then also to do yoga! In this case at first, or even for a while, you will not be able to extend the legs in the upside-down dog, but it does nothing. Yoga for beginners is **a great way to train flexibility.** After all, even in strength or endurance training for each exercise there is a variant that suits you. If you have any difficulties, talk to your instructor and ask him how to proceed. After the initial impact of the first lesson you will learn how to perform the basic exercises and you will realize how yoga, in addition to improving strength and mobility, really makes you feel good. In this discipline there is no rush.

8. **Keep your concentration on body and breathing and give yourself a space to give your thoughts respite**, focusing only on the essential. You may not want to go to a yoga center to spend 60 or 90 minutes on the mat at first and would like to try it here and now. No problem - search online for a fairly simple sequence and try practicing at home for 5, 10, or 15 minutes. Even in this case, however, you will have to identify a lesson suitable for beginners. There will be time for impressive positions and jumps: now is the time to work slowly and precisely. But watch out, because even bending forward or backward can be dangerous for the spine and discs if not done correctly. Beginners practicing yoga at home

should pay double attention and only perform movements that appear "reasonable" at this level.

HOW YOGA SESSION TIPS WORK

1. **Relaxation:** when you arrive in yoga class, the first few minutes are devoted to relaxation. This relaxation allows you to put your worries aside and take a few minutes to let yourself be emptied *(pratyahara)*.

2. **Breathing exercises** *(pranayama)***:** it is a question of observing one's respiratory rhythm and its changes. These exercises are essential for learning to control your breathing, concentrate better and listen less to the mind. The breath is very important in yoga to achieve the postures in full consciousness, to purify the body and the mind.

3. **Preparation for postures:** this is a part devoted to warming up the body by a series of fluid and easy-to-access postures. The best known is that of the sun salutation *(suryanamaskara)*, a succession of twelve postures.

4. **The postures** *(asana)***:** the postures are of course at the heart of the session. They are performed standing, lying down, and sitting with progressive levels of difficulty. It is essential to focus on your breathing and seek the letting go necessary for meditation *(dhyana)*. For example, the triangle position is

performed while standing with legs apart. The student takes a deep breath while raising the arms outstretched horizontally in line with the shoulders. The hips rotate gently so that the right hand rests on the left foot. Maintain the pose, then after several breaths, return to the initial position to repeat the movement with the other arm. There are over 80,000 different postures in yoga.

5. Integration, at the end of the session, with rest: at the end of a yoga session, the body needs a period of respite and mental calm before resuming its usual activity. By lying or sitting, the student can relax the muscles used during the practice one last time and experience a calm body and mind before returning to their daily lives.

YOGA BEGINNERS STYLES

There are several aspects that need to be considered when looking for your style of yoga. The style you practice must be in line with your physical form and with your **psycho-emotional state**. In simple terms, if it is your first yoga class, I do not recommend immersing yourself in an advanced Vinyasa yoga class, because you may think that yoga is not for you, when it may be just the style or level of that specific class. It is also essential to find the teacher with whom to practice that particular style of yoga. Each teacher has their own characteristics and their own personality, which inevitably cannot please everyone, but surely you can find one that satisfies you and that you feel you can trust.

HATHA Yoga

It is a style of yoga with a very relaxed pace that allows you to **listen to your body carefully and slowly.** Static positions are usually performed and maintained for a long time. It allows a greater understanding of the performance and a deep contact with the body. Chanting of mantras, meditation and Breathing techniques (pranyama) can complement the asanas during the class.

VINYASA Yoga Style

It is a dynamic style in which **fluid movements** are performed **combined with the breath.** The inhalation and exhalation phases and the Asanas are performed smoothly and continuously. The term **"vinyasa"** defines the dynamic transition which connects tadasana (the standing position) to AdhoMukhaSvanasana, or the downward facing dog. Often the rhythm is very fast and this does not allow to understand the movements and to listen to the body, especially for beginners.

ASHTANGA Yoga

This style was founded in **1948 by K. Pattabhi Jois** and is a physically demanding practice in which there is a rapid transition connecting the asanas. Each position is preparatory to the next one. The system of ashtanga yoga is based on 6 series of Asanas of increasing difficulty. We will start with the first guided series, until we practice it independently. This self-practice of the first series is commonly called Mysore Style and if practiced in the centers, *teachers' adjustments* can be received.

IYENGAR Yoga

Founded by BKS Iyengar, who developed a style of yoga **focused on alignments.** In this practice, supports are used to achieve the correct training of the asanas. Teacher training takes several years. The classes have a slow pace and are particularly suitable for both beginners and those with physical joint or muscle problems.

KUNDALINI Yoga

It was introduced in the United States by Yoga Bhajan **in 1969,** so it is a fairly recent practice. It is called the **yoga of awareness** and its main purpose is to **awaken and release the healing energy** that is at the base of the spine and then make it rise again. Kundalini yoga classes include chants, mantras, meditations, as well as physical positions, which are however limited in number. It is a very different practice from the others and for this reason sometimes it takes several lessons to get to the heart and be able to wither.

BIKRAM Yoga

In 1971 it was introduced to the United States by Bikram Choundhury. It is a very intense practice in which 26 positions are performed in a heated environment (40 ° C). The sequence includes 45 minutes of standing positions and 45 minutes of floor positions. The purpose of practicing in a heated environment is to improve muscle flexibility and **eliminate toxins from the body.** Before entering a class of this style, it would be useful to already have a basic smattering of body movements in yoga.

HOW TO CHOOSE YOUR STYLE?

After understanding the basic differences between the various styles of yoga, the right question to ask is: *why do I want to practice yoga? What am I looking for? Would I like a more physical practice or am I interested in learning more about meditation techniques?*

Once you have answered these simple questions it will be easier for you to orient yourself and choose a style to practice. Remember that it may be that the style you choose today to start with will no longer be the most suitable for you in a year. You **change, with and through practice,** and sometimes it is necessary to change, experiment, and evolve. But it doesn't always happen like this, sometimes its love at first practice with a style and you always remain faithful to it. Each style has its own characteristics, but they all work mind, body and spirit. Feel free to experiment, **there is no one style better than another.** The right style is the one that allows you to feel your body, experience physical, energetic and mental sensations that make you feel good.

YOGA BEGINNERS EXERCISE

All types of yoga Exercise will allow you to fight against stress and everyone will find in this or that practice the most effective way to reduce their anxiety. But some yoga is particularly recommended for work on the relaxation of the body and the mind.

THE ASANAS, YOGA POSITIONS OF WELL-BEING

The **yoga postures** are called *asanas* and the term is also used to indicate specific sequences that affect multiple locations. The main purpose of the discipline is to stretch the muscles, then to make them strong and reactive with the movements of every day. Asanas help relieve muscle tension, so their practice gives an immediate sense of well-being spreading to the body and expanding to the mind. Let's see together some positions, or asanas, that are easy to practice for those who approach the wonderful world of **yoga for the first time.**

1. Initial relaxation: Relaxation must be practiced at the beginning of each yoga session, as it allows the subject to relax the muscles and become familiar with the individual parts of their body. They are called into question one at a time, deeply perceived and then relaxed one by one. This simple initial exercise also helps to clear the mind of thoughts and stress, as it focuses attention on individual physical sections and thus increases the degree of concentration. It is important that the relaxation is performed in a comfortable and lying position, to allow the limbs to stretch and dissolve in the best possible way.

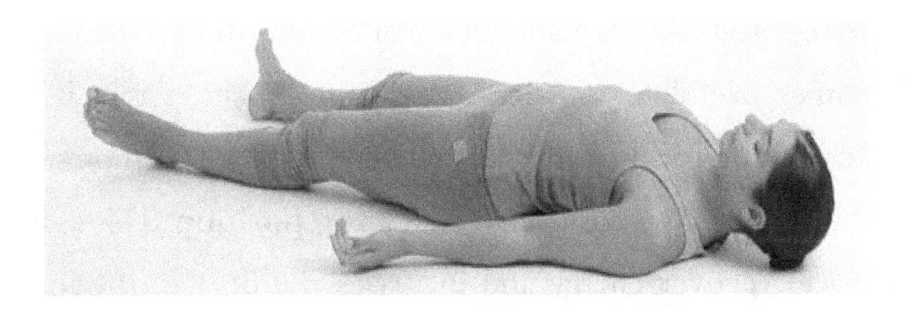

2. The lifting of the legs: This practice does not represent a real asana, but it helps to release tension in the thighs and calves, as well as to **stretch the muscles.** It is performed after an adequate **warm-up of the muscles** by stretching the legs and reaching them with the fingertips, always maintaining a lying position. The length and scope of the exercises depends on the possibilities of the individual subjects and, for no reason, the limbs must be subjected to great strain or muscular tension, especially in the initial stages of learning.

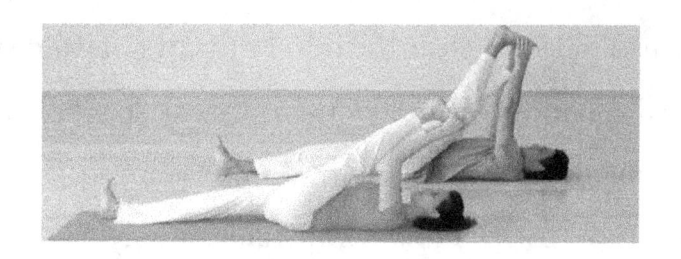

3. Relaxation: Between one exercise and another, yoga requires you to rest and **recover strength**. It therefore becomes useful to practice the 'corpse' position that is to abandon any form of physical resistance for a few moments and let yourself go completely in **a lying position**. This asana helps to recover energy and increases the degree of overall relaxation.

4. The position on the shoulders (Sarvângâsana - Candela): This asana is performed by overturning and raising the legs to the sky. The pressure exerted on the shoulders and neck region favors the functioning of the thyroid gland and helps the blood flow of the lower limbs to flow livelier and more beneficial. This asana must be followed by a moment dedicated to relaxation.

5. The fish (Matsyasana) : This asana proposes an internal curvature of the shoulder blades, performed in a lying position. It is practiced to increase the capacity of the lungs and to improve the flexibility of the upper back.

6. The forward bend (Paschimottanasana) : This asana proposes to stretch the back forward until touching the fingertips with the hands, keeping the back very

low. Beneficial for the **lower back**, this asana massages the abdominal organs and **helps the digestive system** to energize itself, thus fighting episodes related to constipation and gastric reflux.

7. The triangle (trikonasa) : This simple asana is performed **standing** . Keep the legs apart and touch the toe of the right foot with the right hand, extending the left limb in a horizontal position. The sequence is then repeated with the other limb.

8. The final relaxation: as happens at the beginning of **the yoga session**, also at the end it is necessary to perform a complete relaxation, which allows you to establish a relationship of confidence with the individual parts of the body and to thank them for the yield they have offered us during exercise.

YOGA POSITION/POSTURE FOR BEGINNER

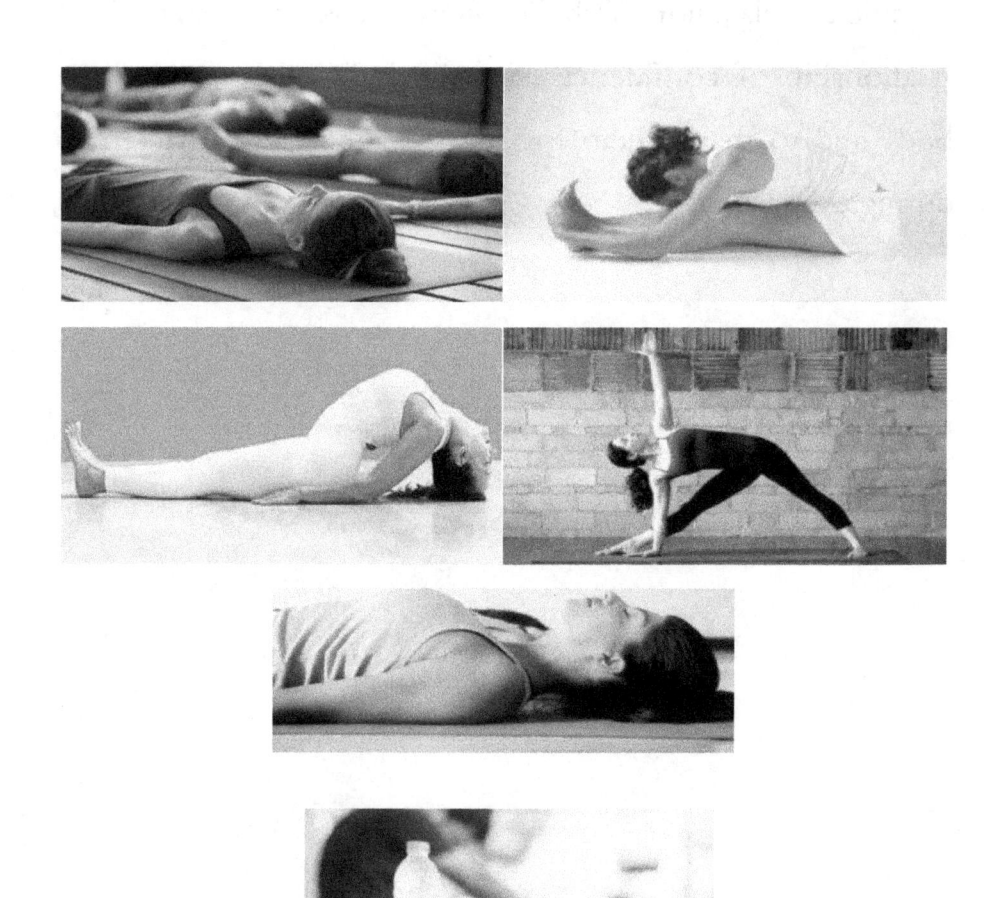

The above diagrams are examples of YOGA Position for beginners. And these can help every beginner to have a starting yoga posture

Yoga is said to have as **many postures as there are living beings.** In general, today there are 84 asanas, of which 32 are essential and 12 are defined as the **queen positions of yoga** because they allow you to work on the whole Body. In a beginner class, we focus in particular on the queen positions and their variants, then trying to customize the practice according to the students and their level of advancement. During a lesson you will have the opportunity to perform at least one position for each group of asanas that follow:

Standing postures: Standing postures are often done first in a yoga class to "increase the heat" and for warm up. In vinyasa / flow style yoga, standing poses are tied together to form long sequences. In hatha lessons, the standing poses can instead be performed individually with a rest phase between one posture and the other.

Balance Positions: These positions for yoga beginners are an important way to build the strength needed to be able to perform more advanced postures later. While they may seem difficult at first, you will find that you can improve dramatically with regular practice.

Beginners Yoga: Balance Positions

Back bends: As a beginner, you will generally begin with a slight flexion and extension of the spine, then progress to deeper positions. Since we rarely move this way in daily life, back bends are essential for the health and longevity of the spine.

Seated Positions: Seated stretches, which often focus on stretching the hips and hamstrings, are usually done towards the end of a yoga class after the body is warm. Placing a folded blanket or block under your butt is a good way to feel more comfortable in these postures.

Resting or Supine Positions: It is important to know the resting poses, especially the baby pose, which you are encouraged to do whenever you need a break during a yoga session. These resting positions continue the body work initiated by the sitting postures, as well as providing a slight back flexion, twist and inversion. Among these positions we also find Savasana, or the position of the corpse, which recalls the final relaxation of the body and mind.

Natural ways to strengthen your body

The following pose can help to strengthen your body naturally

1. Warm Up Pose

Start with the Plank pose, that is, the palms of the hands should remain flat on the floor just below the shoulder and the legs stretched back, forming a straight line similar to an axis. Take a deep breath and lift your hips off the ground, lean on your hands and heels. The head should be oriented towards the ground, repeat the deep breath a couple of times while holding the position. Now slowly lower your body, sliding your hands back so that your palms rest next to your chest. The toes should touch the mat. Take another deep breath, push your palm firmly, and lift your chest, neck, and head to slide. Stretch your legs and shoulders and take 5 deep breaths, after exhaling while lowering your head, chest and head down. Then bring your hands in front of you, while your palms press firmly on the mat. Inhale deeply while balancing on the palm of your hand, push your body away from the mat, balancing on your feet, and shift from dog to low pose.

2. Bhujangasana - Cobra Pose:

Lie on your back on the mat; keep your legs straight with your heels touching. Place your hands next to your chest with your palms facing the floor. Inhale deeply as you push your neck, chest, and head back into balance. Exhale deeply and return to the starting position.

This exercise mainly stimulates and strengthens the digestive system, eliminates the flaccidity of the stomach and improves the flexibility of the spine.

3. Dhanurasana - Bow Pose:

Lie in a prone position, with your hands elongated and your legs stretched out in the back. Bend your knees and bring your feet toward your heels. Take a deep breath and extend your hands back to support your ankles, while lifting your chest and head and keeping your head tilted slightly back.

Try to stretch your body as far back as possible, without the back-feeling pressure, forming an arch with our body. Take 10 breaths holding the position until all the air is released, relax until you return to the starting position. This exercise will help you strengthen your abdominal organs as well as strengthen your back and circulatory system. Finally, it strengthens the white blood cells and helps us feel healthy and have a strong immune system.

This yoga posture has the objective of improving the immune system, helping the body to fight against external pathogenic aggression and infections. Lie down with your back on the mat, hands long and palms facing the floor. Bend your knees so that they form a 90 degree angle. Take a breath while moving your hips and chest up, exhale slowly while trying to keep your body relaxed.

4. Setu Bhandasana - Bridge Pose:

This yoga posture has the objective of improving the immune system, helping the body to fight against external pathogenic aggression and infections. Lie down with your back on the mat, hands long and palms facing the floor. Bend your knees so that they form a 90-degree angle. Take a breath while moving your hips and chest up, exhale slowly while trying to keep your body relaxed.

5. Ardha Chakrasana - Half Wheel Pose:

Lie on your back on the mat, your heels should be oriented parallel to the floor and hip width apart, as close to the bone seat as possible. Gradually balance your head with your feet, breathing deeply, pushing the body up, without putting pressure on the neck. Breathe out and slowly lower your body back to the starting position.

Natural Way To Calm Your Mind

Using the yoga Savasana position of a dead body, it is one of the most important Asanas to reach a state of relaxation and if performed correctly, you will see all forms of anxiety disappear.

1. Lie on the ground on a mat, with your arms at your sides about 20 cm from your body, palms facing up. If you feel uncomfortable with your head on the ground, you can put a thin pillow or a folded blanket under your head.

2. Slightly separate your feet into a comfortable position and close your eyes.

3. Become aware of the right hand and relax it, then the right wrist, elbow, armpit, right hip, right buttock, right thigh, right knee, calf, heel, sole of the foot and relax them one by one.

4. Repeat the process with the left side of the body, then with the head and torso area.

5. Make sure that each part of the body is completely relaxed, as if it is merging with the floor. You can repeat the process several times, in this way you eliminate any tension.

6. The head and spine must be in a straight line, make sure the head does not fall to the side or back, keep the chin towards the sternum.

7. Become aware of the natural breath and let it become relaxed.

8. To keep the mind from wandering focus on the breath, if you do not use a mantra, do the breath count: Start counting your breaths from 27 to zero. Repeat mentally "I am inhaling 27", "I am exhaling 27", I am inhaling 26, I am exhaling 26 and so on until zero.

9. To promote relaxation you can also help yourself by covering your eyes with something or by turning off the light.

10. You can choose the duration of the practice according to the available time you have, the longer it is, the better the results.

11. If you lose your breath count, because you are out of focus or some thought has distracted you, start counting again from 27.

12. While doing the practice, if you feel some pain or tension in one or more areas of the body, focus on these. First observe the discomfort, that pain, if images or other things come to you, without judging then imagine breathing with the painful areas, in this way it is as if you were communicating with your body that expresses the blocks, the tensions contained in the specific areas.

13. Breathing through them helps you release both physical, mental and emotional tensions that have become stuck in that area of the body, recharging them with energy.

THE YOGA SAVASANA BENEFITS

Here, in summary, are the main benefits of Savasana. Savasana Physical benefits include:

1. Gives vitality
2. Stimulates blood circulation
3. Improves sleep disorders
4. Relieves migraines, constipation, indigestion and lower back pain
5. Regulates the heartbeat
6. Helps to control high blood pressure

Emotional benefits:

1. Reduces stress
2. Gives inner peace
3. Counteracts anxiety and depression

Spiritual benefits:

1. Develops awareness of the body and mind
2. Develops self-awareness
3. It represents a door to inner knowledge.

Savasana is an unbelievable posture. Seemingly very simple, it induces you into a state of deep relaxation that will help you calm your spirit, relax your body and increase your focus and awareness.

GENTLE POSES FOR RELAXATION AND HEALING

YOGA POSES FOR RELAXATION

Yoga is based on correct relaxation, breathing, and meditation. Practicing it brings many benefits such as calming anxiety and stress. Here are five exercises to help you relax, even when you have little free time.

Sukhasana

This is one of the most common and simple yoga postures, ideal for those who do not have a lot of flexibility. If you already have experience, it can work as a warm-up for muscles and joints to later do more complex ones.

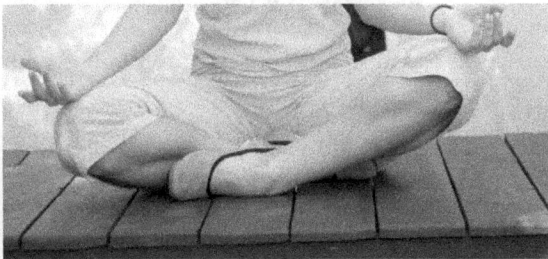

How to do it:

stretch out your *Widemat,* the yoga mat, and sit with your legs and spine stretched and straight, take a deep breath and cross your legs. Place your hands on your knees, palms up, without pressure.

Savasana

A simple position, but one of the most effective to relax or to control thoughts in difficult moments. For experts it is useful to end a session with this posture so that the body relaxes after stretching.

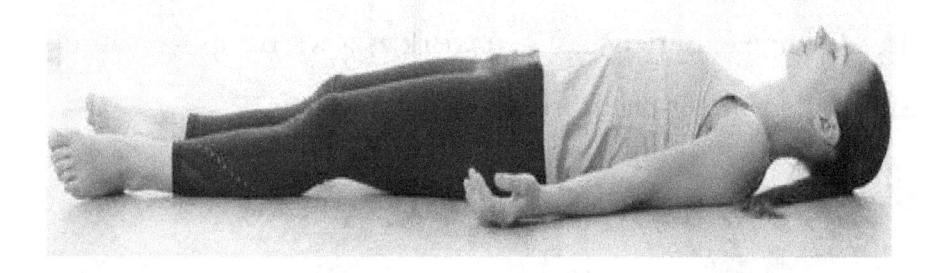

How to do it:

Lie down on your *Widemat,* stretching your entire body. Spread your legs and arms slightly. Place your hands palms up. Close your eyes and take a deep breath.

Padmasana

This posture is one of the best known and most emblematic of yoga, as well as the most useful for relaxing because it is ideal for doing breathing exercises that help clear the mind and focus on breathing.

How to do it:

Sit on the *Widemat* with your back straight and legs straight. Bend one leg, grab your foot and place it on the opposite thigh, closest to the hip. Bend the other leg and do the same, place your foot on top of the other thigh. Regarding your hands, place them on your knees and in each one, join your index finger with your thumb.

Balasana

This position also helps a lot to relax because it allows you to rest your back and discharge all the energy and stress that falls on it. It is also used to start a yoga session.

How to do it:

Kneel on your *Widemat*, knees hip-width apart. Sit back on your heels, with your toes together. Take a deep breath and lean your back forward as far as you can, until your forehead hits the ground. Make sure your body is relaxed by doing stretching or breathing exercises before doing it.

Vrkasasana

Besides being a relaxation method, it is also used to work on balance. To carry it out, it is important to have a relaxed body and a calm mind, as well as a lot of practice.

How to do it:

Start with your feet hip-width apart. Take a deep breath and be aware of your body weight. Then, fixate on a distant point and shift the weight to the right leg, lift the left foot and rest it on the inner aspect of the right

thigh. With your palms together, raise your arms as high as you can. Try to stretch your back.

YOGA: HEALING THROUGH ASANAS

We know that yoga is a great physical practice: it tones the body, stimulates flexibility and promotes relaxation. But it is also an extremely powerful emotional practice. We tend to retain past emotions and trauma in our bodies. Any heartache, anguish, or trial that we have experienced, but have not felt deeply, can easily make its home within our bodies.

Yoga is a very useful tool to help remove these toxic energies and find true healing, from the inside out.

1. Long Holds: Learning to Feel

When we hold *asanas* (poses) for long periods of time, feelings begin to bubble within us. Especially as we focus our focus inward, we become more aware of what is happening within. Holding poses for a long time activates our feelings and emotions. We start tuning in and we really feel what is coming. As we continue our practice, we will notice that specific postures have more tension than others. They are likely to be the same ones that will help us **feel** and **heal** Most.

Pose: *Mandukasana* (Frog Pose)

This deep hip opener is a great place to start. We carry a lot of tension in our hips and the frog pose is quick to warn us.

This pose can become very uncomfortable. See if you can handle the discomfort.

One breath at a time. It is important to note that discomfort and pain are two different things: Get out of the pose if you feel any pain.

2. Grounding: Mind-Body Connection

Establishing a strong mind-body connection is one of the first steps in healing past trauma. To heal, we must learn to look within. Yoga helps us do this because it gives us a safe place to explore the sensations in our bodies. As we practice more to notice what is happening inside, we begin to notice more emotions arising. Grounding poses help us form a powerful mind-body connection because we are both in our bodies but at the same time supported by the ground. They give us space to feel and be held simultaneously.

Pose: *SuptaBaddhaKonasana* (Reclining Bound Angle Pose)

Supta Baddha Konasana is a good place to land while fully relaxing on the mat. Place one hand on your heart and one hand on your belly to keep your attention on your breathing and the present moment.

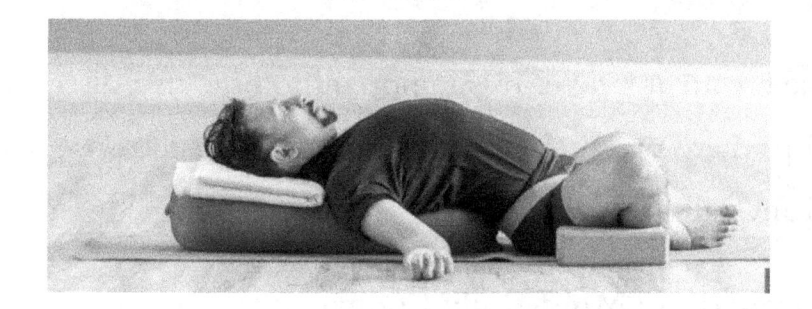

3. Surrender: Emotional Release

Sometimes all we really need to heal is letting go. Unfortunately, letting go has become a cliché in yoga bubbles. However, letting go does not necessarily mean releasing pain or anger, sometimes it means surrendering to it; letting go of it. We often resist feelings that don't feel "right." But in reality, feelings are neither good nor bad. They just are. And feeling them is not what is painful. It is our resistance to feelings that causes us pain. So sometimes we just have to surrender to our feelings to heal them completely.

Pose: *EkaPadaRajakapotasana* (Half-dove Pose)

Pigeon pose is a great place to get carried away. Because our hips carry so many emotions, when we open them deeply, we often have no choice but to give up. If you find yourself crying a lot at Pigeon, that's completely normal. By holding this posture for a long period, we break through those walls that we have built around past trauma and often release them by crying. This is very healing.

4. Heart Openers: Vulnerability

Have you ever experienced a 'light bulb moment' in a yoga class? As if you suddenly realized why you have felt in a specific way for so long.

Yoga helps us to deepen and be very vulnerable. Vulnerability is essential to our healing. When we cannot be vulnerable, we begin to exclude people. We build walls around our hearts as a form of "protection" when all we are really doing is harming ourselves. We must be able to open our hearts to find self-love, healing, and ultimately love others completely. The opening postures of the heart help us to do exactly that. By physically opening our hearts, we send a signal to our inner heart to open as well.

Pose: UrdhvaDhanurasana (Wheel Pose)

Wheel is a deep heart opener that helps us tear down those walls and learn to open our hearts. This is a great pose because we are opening our hearts but we have our hands and feet on the ground while keeping us grounded.

5. Balance: Responding vs. Reacting

Very often, when we get angry, we **react** rather than **respond**. Reactions turn into regrets. We snap and don't take a moment to think, or even breathe, before we speak and end up hurting someone else or ourselves.

Yoga creates a space for us to learn to respond to tense or unfortunate situations with equanimity. Responding to these situations rather than reacting generally results in a more calm and friendly interaction. And we will most likely walk away from them feeling better than if we had reacted.

Pose: *Natarajasana* (Dancer Pose)

Balancing poses help us learn how to respond. When we fall from a balancing pose, like Dancer, we have two options: we can get angry and frustrated that we fell, or we can take a deep breath, maybe even smile, and do it again.

6. Ahimsa : Non-violence

Ahimsa translates from Sanskrit to "non-violence". It is inspired by the concept that all living things are sacred and therefore should not be harmed.

This also applies to you. We talk a lot about being nice to others, but sometimes we forget about ourselves. Just as we should treat others with kindness and compassion, we should treat ourselves in the same way. Many of us tend to be very hard on ourselves. Whether it's the way we look, how smart we are, or our general position in life. Think about how you talk to yourself when you make a mistake. Would you talk to your best friend in the same way? Yoga teaches us to be gentle with ourselves. They teach us to rest when we need to and to listen to our bodies. When we learn how to do this both on and off the mat, we become more in tune with our feelings and emotions, and we understand that we must be kind to ourselves to heal and find self-love.

Pose: *Balasana* (Child's Pose)

Often all it takes is a return to basics. The child's posture serves many purposes, one of which is as a resting place.

7. Self-empowerment: courage

Finally, to heal past trauma, we must bring our inner power to life. This is not aggressive or controlling power, this is empowerment. It is confidence, courage, truth; It is a willingness to appear in your life.

Self-empowerment is a place where you recognize your path and don't run from it. Instead, you embrace it. And you embrace all that you are: strengths and flaws alike.

Pose: Warrior 2 helps us dive deep into our power. Create a fire in our legs and a feeling of freedom in our hearts. The excessive demands of mind and psyche are now held responsible as the main cause of illnesses and everyday complaints such as headaches and sleep disorders. But how can yoga promote healing and how exactly does the body and mind benefit?

DIFFERENT WAYS TO REACH SAME DESTINATION IN YOGA

Yoga is one but there are different types, we can define them as different ways to reach the same destination, the five most important ones are:

1. KARMA-YOGA > The path of action.
2. BHAKTI-YOGA > The path of devotion and love.
3. JÑANA YOGA > The path of inquiry and discernment.
4. RAJA-YOGA > The path of introspection.
5. HATHA YOGA > The path of balance of internal energies

KARMA YOGA – THE PART OF ACTION

Karma yoga is the first of the Vedic methods recommended for self-realization. It is the path of selfless action in which one does one's duty without expecting any reward. By sacrificing the fruits of one's actions to God, one is not bound by karma and one develops equanimity. This is the whole purpose of Karma yoga. This book presents Karma yoga in a simple and comprehensive way.

What Is The Role Of Karma Yoga In *Sadhana*?

Sadhguru: It is not needed really. Yoga does not need karma. Yoga is to go beyond karma.

Why karma yoga has been brought in is to bring about balance in a person. Whatever we call as our awareness, our love, our experience or our glimpses of our reality, if it has to be sustained, the path of non-doing is a very wonderful path, but it is very slippery. Extremely slippery. It is the simplest and the most difficult. It is not difficult but it is not at all easy, because it is simple – right now, here and now. But that here and now – how to get it? Whatever you do, it is not in your hands. It is never going to be in your hands. But your hands need something right now, you need to hold on to something. That is why the crutch of karma yoga. Without the crutch, most people will not be able to walk. There are a few beings who can walk without the crutch from the first moment. They are very rare beings. Everyone else needs the crutch to manage your awareness. Without this, most people are incapable of remaining aware. So karma yoga is brought into your life to properly temper sadhana with the right kind of action.

Karma yoga has unfortunately been described as service, but it is not so. It is a way of undoing the impressions that you have gathered. If you can joyfully involve yourself in any activity, that is karma yoga. If you do it with great effort, only karma will come, no yoga will happen.

Generally, it is through various activities that you perform that you get entangled and enmeshed with life. But if the activity becomes a process of liberation instead of entanglement, it is karma yoga. Whether it is work or walking on the street or talking to someone, the nature of the activity is not important. When you do something only because it is needed, where it does not mean anything to you but you are capable of involving yourself as if that is your life, it transforms you and action becomes liberating. When we were building the Dhyanalinga, people thought, "This is it! He wants this to happen. Let us do it! Once this is done, we can relax." They worked like their life depended on it. They went from house to house, raising funds and bringing the necessary support and made it happen. I will always keep it on because people need that kind of action. They need to do what is needed without worrying about their fulfillment and their likes and dislikes.

Anyway we are doing something for our growth, so let us do something that is useful to everyone. Let us take sensible action. There have been many masters who created action like this. When Gurdjieff started his centers in Europe, the European elite went to him. In the morning he would give them a shovel and a pickaxe and tell them, "Dig trenches." In the hot sun, they stood and dug and dug. These were not people who are used to labor of any kind. By the time they had worked a few hours, they had blisters all over. He stood there and drove them on. By late evening, they were hungry but they worked and worked, digging trenches. Then he would look at the watch, "Okay, it is seven o'clock. Looks like dinner time. All of you can close the trenches again before we go for dinner." A whole day's work! Doing something that does not mean anything to you with total involvement is what breaks the karmic structure. Karma means action. If action has to become yoga, action should be liberating. If your activity has become a process of binding yourself, it is karma. So the question is not about how much activity you do. How you are performing the activity is what makes the difference. If you are crawling through your work, that is karma. If you are dancing through your work, that is karma yoga.

Bhakti-Yoga - The Path Of Devotion And Love.

The term *bhakti* derives from the Sanskrit root *bhaj* (to participate) and is translated as "devotion" or "love" towards something that cannot be defined in an immediately perceptible being and therefore an unconditional love of a spiritual nature. More precisely, it is an expression of *bhavana*, that is, that condition by which the heart (the emotions) of the devotee predisposes itself to an exquisitely mystical relationship with the cosmic consciousness. A new spiritual philosophy that is introduced with the Bhagavad Gita announces the possibility granted to human nature to experience the divine in a pre-representative dimension through an emotional experience, this approach is precisely that of *bhakti yoga*. This article aims to provide the reader with a methodological and historical framework to grasp the birth and the reasons for the spread of devotional yoga through the centuries until it is able to find space also in the West of the twentieth century.

Bhaktiyoga

A precise analysis of the form of *bhakti, shows* how the yoga connected to it is divided into two moments: the first involves the renunciation of the fruit of actions in a psychological process that leads to the progressive dis-identification with one's ordinary identity; the second is to take up abode in Krishna with the fiery devotion that changes the grueling sacrifices of *tapas* into the more accessible renunciations of bhakti. The whole universe is contained in the inner eye of the faithful who, seeing only the person of Krishna, spontaneously associates the universe itself with this. This vision involves an unusual physiological and affective state where the straightening of the hair is described (*hrstaroman*) and unbridled joy. The liberation desired by the yogi is, in this perspective, the ecstatic experience of the god. In this regard, it should be emphasized how the ecstatic condition can be observed with the gaze of the natural sciences without the intervention of the metaphysical narrative. The ability to have an ecstatic experience is inherent in human beings and is evident from the fact that ordinary consciousness does not present itself as rigidly structured. Sleep is the first and most evident empirical proof of what is asserted here but there is also ecstasy or trance that allows the consciousness to change to pass to a condition where the bodily experience, the categories of space and time, are perceived as radically different from the ordinary waking condition. In traditional cultures the search for ecstasy took place and occurs through the consumption of psychotropic substances capable of altering the central nervous system and consequently the senses of the person. The music and the dances assisted by the rhythmic sounds produced by the drums can produce similar and healthier effects since in such cases there are external stimuli and physiological alterations connected to them. In this regard, it is worth noting the research of D. Zappatore, Dhikr: psycho-physiology of ecstasy in Sufi mysticism. The text highlights the hypothesis of the production of endorphins which would be activated by acoustic and visual stimulations; once synthesized, these substances transmit the nerve impulse and have the ability to activate or inhibit the receptor sites present in adjacent cells.

Diffusion of bhakti

Between the sixth and tenth centuries, the south of India was crossed by chanters of Krishna, the supreme *avatar* of Vishnu, who in ecstatic condition attract the attention of the people with their incessant repetition of devotional prayers and mantras accompanied by the *mridanga* drum whose rhythm, as seen, favors the physiological condition of ecstasy. In Bengal the Vishnu devotional practice spreads relentlessly, placing the Lord as a reference for every cosmic manifestation and in the play (*lila*) of bliss, Radha gets confused and lost in Krishna. *Tantra* and *jnana* elements between the 10th and 15th centuries they intersect with the devotion that in the sixteenth century regains its original autonomous strength through the work of the bard Chaitanya who brings the cult of Visnu back to the center through processional practices of ecstatic singers at the incessant repetition of the *maha mantra*. *"Hare kṛṣṇa hare kṛṣṇa kṛṣṇa kṛṣṇa hare hare hare rama hare rama rama rama hare hare"* is the great mantra of Upanisadic origin later brought to the West by the teaching of Bhakti-Vedānta Svāmī Prabhupāda. The bhakti culture remains present until the contemporary age through the Bengali mystic Ramakrishna (1834 - 1886) and his most famous disciple Swami Vivekananda (1863 - 1902); they prefer paths where devotion to Krishna does not excel - the first will follow every religious path preferring devotion to Kali while the second will be above all a *karma yogi* - but both recognize in traditional bhakti a path of absolute importance for the knowledge of the god. We are in 1965 when a sixty-nine-year-old man from Calcutta arrives in New York to found a mission and to promulgate the teachings of Chaitanya centered on the maha *mantra*, the man is Bhaktivedanta Swami Prabhupada, aka Abhay Charan De (1896-1977). Prabhupada founds ISKCON, the International Society for Krishna Consciousness, which, among mixed fortunes, survives both in India and in the West to the present day.

Jñana Yoga : The Path Of Inquiry And Discernment.

What is Jnana Yoga?

Jnana is Sanskrit for "knowledge or wisdom" and Jnana Yoga is the path of attaining knowledge of the true nature of reality through the practice of meditation, self-inquiry, and contemplation. Jnana Yoga can be defined as the "awareness of absolute consciousness," and is a comprehensive practice of self-study (Svadhyaya).

In Jnana yoga, the mind is used to inquire into its own nature and to transcend the mind's identification with its thoughts and ego. The fundamental goal of Jnana yoga is to become liberated from the illusionary world of maya (self-limiting thoughts and perceptions) and to achieve the union of the inner Self (Atman) with the oneness of all life (Brahman). This is achieved by steadfastly practicing the mental techniques of self-questioning, reflection and conscious illumination that are defined in the Four Pillars of Knowledge. Jnana Yoga utilizes a one-pointed meditation on a single question of self-inquiry to remove the veils of illusion created by your concepts, world views, and perceptions. This practice allows you to realize the temporary and illusionary nature of *maya* and to see the oneness of all things.

"Jnana Yoga, or the science of the Self, is not a subject that can be understood and realized through mere intellectual study, reasoning, discussion or arguments. It is the most difficult of all sciences." – Swami Sivananda

Prerequisites of Jnana Yoga

The Four Pillars of Knowledge (sadhana chatushtaya) are the prescribed steps toward achieving liberation in Jnana Yoga. These practices build upon each other and thus should be practiced in sequential order. Even if one does not have the goal of achieving liberation, practicing these techniques will cultivate spiritual insight and understanding as well as reduce one's suffering and dissatisfaction of life.

1. Viveka (discernment, discrimination) is a deliberate, continuous intellectual effort to distinguish between the real and the unreal, the permanent and the temporary, and the Self and not-Self.

2. Vairagya (dispassion, detachment) is cultivating non-attachment or indifference toward the temporal objects of worldly possessions and the ego-mind. "It is only when the mind is absolutely free from the attachment of all sorts that true knowledge begins to dawn." – Swami Sivananda.

3. Shatsampat (six virtues) are six mental practices to stabilize the mind and emotions, and to further develop the ability to see beyond the illusions of maya.

>•**Shama** (tranquility, calmness) is the ability to keep the mind peaceful, through moderating its reaction to external stimuli.

>• **Dama** (restraint, control) is the strengthening of the mind to be able to resist the control of the senses, and

the training of the senses to be used only as instruments of the mind.

•**Uparati** (withdrawal, renunciation) is the abandonment of all activities that are not one's Dharma (Duty). A simple lifestyle is followed that contains no worldly distractions from the spiritual path.

• **Titiksha** (endurance, forbearance) is the tolerance of external non-conducive situations that are commonly considered to produce suffering, especially in extreme opposite states (success and failure, hot and cold, pleasure and pain).

• **Shraddha** (faith, trust) is a sense of certainty and belief in one's guru (teacher), the scriptures and the yogic path.

• **Samadhana** (focus, concentration) is the complete one-pointedness of the mind.

4. **Mumukshutva** (longing, yearning) is an intense and passionate desire for achieving the liberation from suffering. In order to achieve liberation, one must be completely

committed to the path, with such longing that all other desires fade away.

How to practice Jnana Yoga

It can be difficult to grasp or comprehend the intellectual approach of jnana yoga, and since one can easily overemphasize intellectual attainment it is important to cultivate humility and compassion on this path. It is easy to become entangled in the constructs and thoughts of the mind and lose sight of the goal of jnana: to realize the divine oneness inherent in all beings.

Recommended that one practice Hatha Yoga, Karma Yoga and Bhakti Yoga as prerequisites. These yogic practices will prepare and purify the body, mind, and heart for the rigors of Jnana Yoga.

Once you have attained some advancement in the other yogas, begin practicing the four pillars of knowledge. You do not need to feel you have mastered one pillar before moving on to the next, but do resist the temptation to progress forward before you are ready. This is considered an advanced practice and thus would be contraindicated for anyone with a history of mental disease or emotional instability. Working with a qualified teacher or guru is highly recommended to accurately assess your progress, offer individual instruction, and provide guidance for your progression.

Three Core Practices Of Jnana Yoga

After one has studied and successfully practiced the four pillars, then you are considered ready to begin the three core practices of Jnana Yoga. These Upanishadic teachings include sravana or "hearing," manana or "reflection," and nididhyasana or "meditation". These lead to Atma-Sakshatkara or direct realization.

| 1. Tree | 2. Triangle | 3. Downward dog | 4. Cobra | 5. Locust |

| 7. Bow | 7. Posterior stretch | 7. Spinal twist | 8. Plow | 11. Fish | 12. Corpse |

- **Sravana** is the hearing or experiencing the sacred knowledge in the ancient Vedic texts of the Upanishad. Usually, a teacher or guru will guide the yogi through discussions on the philosophy of non-dualism. In this stage, the student should read and study the Upanishads and achieve a deep understanding of the concepts of Atman and Brahman and the philosophy of non-dualism.

- **Manana** is the thinking and reflecting on these teachings of non-duality. The student is expected to spend many hours thinking and contemplating on the various ideas of svadhyaya and sravana.

- **Nididhyasana** is the constant and profound meditation on the inner Self. This involves the meditation and reflection on the real meaning of the Maha-Vakyas, the primary mantras or "Great Sayings" of the Upanishads. Through the continuous focus on these seeds of wisdom, a yogi can obtain the union of thought and action, knowing and being.

Raja Yoga - The Path Of Introspection.

It is the so-called royal yoga, the one that focuses on mental energy, awareness and self-realization. Raja Yoga is the opposite of Hatha yoga (more physical), the sublime method to detach oneself from the material, from one's ego and from everyday life. Considered to be the supreme yoga in India, **Raja yoga** (where *raja* means *"royal"*) is opposed to the better known Hatha yoga. In fact, if the latter focuses on the physical body, on asanas and breathing, Raja yoga focuses on the mind, on the development of mental energy and on self-awareness.

The principles of Raja yoga are exposed in the **Yoga Sutras**, a work attributed to the Indian philosopher **Patañjali** : they are **196 sutras** , that is to say short sentences designed to be memorized easily and to pass on knowledge among people.

The purpose of Raja yoga is **self-realization** after embarking on a path that allows you to free yourself from your desires as a source of suffering, or from everyday problems that distract from the true purpose of earthly life, that is, the search for one's inner self. Already living showing gratitude for what one has, and not continuing to desire what one does not have, is an important step towards awareness and a certain predisposition aimed at achieving the union of body, mind and spirit.

The 8 Stages Of Raja Yoga

However, whenever you hear about Raja yoga, you are likely to hear about the 8 stages, through which man can learn to discipline his mind and unite it with body and spirit, with the aim of achieving the concept of "unique".

The 8 Stages of Raja Yoga are:

> ➤ **Yama (abstinence):**

They are the moral basis of yoga, the necessary prerequisite for real progress in the following stages. The Yama are 5 and can be interpreted as the beginning of the path of the practitioner and mainly concerns the behavior towards others: Ahimsa (non-violence), Satya (truth), Asteya (not stealing), Brahmacharya (self-retention), Aparigraha (not avarice).

> ➤ **Niyama (observances):**

These are the behaviors to follow for those engaged in the path of yoga. They concern behavior towards oneself and include purification precepts, hygiene rules and correct mental attitudes.

There are 5 Niyamas : Saucha (purity), Santosha (contentment), Tapas (austerity), Svadhyaya (individual study), Ishvaraparanidhana (abandonment to God).

➤ Asanas (positions):

These are the postures of yoga , which help the body and strengthen it, improving its balance and elasticity. They are the starting point to learn about yoga and to deepen its practice with Pranayama and Dhyana .

➤ Pranayama (control of prana):

Constitutes the set of techniques for controlling the vital force (prana), through breathing exercises.

➤ Pratyahara (control of the senses):

Consists in the withdrawal of the mind from sensitive objects. It refers to the idea of pulling the senses away from any objects of desire, pulling them inward and developing a strong sense of internalization.

➢ Dharana (concentration):

Constitutes the first level of concentration. Patanjali describes concentration as the ability to "bind consciousness in one place". Dharana can be practiced towards an object to draw attention to and determines the absorption of mental energies in a single point.

➢ Dhyana (meditation):

It means observing reality for what it is, without prejudice and conditioning. It means perceiving the qualitative aspects of the object of meditation, beyond the form. It is the state of profound peace that is achieved when the mind calms down while remaining alert.

➢ Samadhi (ecstasy, bliss):

It is the supreme stage of yoga, in which one connects with the Absolute. It is that state of total coherence with oneself and life that the human being can reach after transforming everything that limits him. It occurs when the mind focuses on its own meditation object and becomes one with it. Here then is the sought-after union and the realization of yoga.

HATHA-YOGA: PHYSICAL YOGA

The word HATHA is made up of two words: HA which means SUN and THA which means MOON? We can describe the Sun and the Moon as two energies represented within our body as the vital force and the mental force. By joining these two energies and reaching balance through the practice of Yoga, the spiritual energy called Kundalini can be awakened. In the practice of this type of Yoga, the physical part is worked, the body is given harmony and balance; this harmony and balance reaches our mind reaching a mental tranquility.

Within Hatha-Yoga there are a series of practices that are described below.

Internal Purification : Shatkarmas

Breathing exercises : Pranayama

Postures : Asanas

Energy Keys : Bandhas

Psychic Gestures : Mudras

SHATKARMAS: NETI, THE NASAL SHOWER

Shatkarmas are internal purification techniques, there are 6 different techniques and NETI is one of the nasal cleansing procedures.

In Yoga, inspiration and expiration is through the nostrils and it is here that we capture the vital energy, for this reason, the nostrils have to be kept clean so that the air / energy can be carried out optimally. Dirt and mucus accumulate in the nostrils, these residues should eliminated by blowing.

These are some of the benefits:

Facilitates and improves nasal breathing, as waste is eliminated from the nostrils.

Increases resistance against colds, having them free of bacteria.

PRANAYAMA: THE BREATH

When we are born, our first contact with life we do it through an inspiration and this life ends with an expiration, this is the key to life and for this reason it is so important that we have good quality breath.

Based on this good quality of breathing we can say that this will be the quality of our life. We can describe that there are four types of breaths:

1. Abdominal or diaphragmatic breathing: It is the breathing of babies when they are asleep

2. Thoracic or rib breathing: It is what is usually done when practicing gymnastics.

3. Clavicular or high breathing: When we have problems, states of tension, nerves or anxiety, the breath that comes out, when we are in some of these states, the solar plexus remains contracted and pulmonary ventilation is poor.

4. Complete yogic breathing: This is the most complicated of the breaths since it naturally costs a lot and we have to do it more consciously. It is the most efficient and complete breathing since the lungs take in more oxygen and expel all the stale air. When we practice this breath we are practicing the three previous breaths.

Example of Pranayama Yoga exercises

ASANAS: POSTURES

We can describe Asanas as static and dynamic exercises that their performance influences our body. How is an asana different from a gymnastic exercise? In attention, attitude; Asana is performed under internal listening, an observation to recognize how our interior is and through this method we can listen to what our body and mind tell us and how each of the asanas that we do come to influence us.

Asana posture example

ASANAS

Tadasana — Vrkasana — Utthita Trikonasana — Utthita Parsvakonasana — Virabhadrasana I

Virabhadrasana II — Parsvotanasana — Prasarita Padotanasana — Urdhva Prasarita Padotanasana — Vajrasana

Bharadvajasana — Sarvangasana — Halasana — Viparita — Savasana

Bandhas: Energy Keys

A bandha can be defined as a contraction of an area of our body and that has its repercussions on our body both organically, energetically and mentally.

We can describe three bandhas: Jalandhara Bandha, Uddiyana Bandha and Mula Bandha. Mudras are symbolic signs that are generally performed with the hands, just like bandhas we can define them as energy seals, which direct energy to all areas of the body. Mudras are used both in the practice of Yoga and in meditation as they help us to internalize and concentrate.

The Eight Limbs of Yoga

Yoga sutras are also called "Yoga of the 8 limbs" or Asthanga yoga precisely because Patanjali has identified in 8 stages (or "*anga*") the way to reach the ultimate goal of yoga, that is the cessation of mental afflictions.

These 8 stages are:

- Yama - Abstinence
- Nyama - Observances
- Asana - Positions
- Pranayama - Techniques for absorbing vital energy (breathing)
- Pratyahara - Withdrawal of sensory perceptions

- Dharana - Concentration

- Dyana - Meditation

- Samadhi - Enlightenment, bliss

Patanjali created a coherent Yoga practice consisting of eight limbs, which serve as guidelines for living a meaningful and purposeful life and serve as a prescription for moral and ethical conduct and self-discipline. The limbs also direct our attention to our health and help us to acknowledge the spiritual aspects of our nature and assist us in living a life of balance and connectedness. The eight limbs of Yoga are as follows: the yamas, the niyamas, asana, pranayama, pratyahara, dharana, dhyana, and Samadhi. The yamas and niyamas, the first and second limbs of Yoga, respectively, are Principles for living that incorporate morality or ethics, concentration or meditation, and wisdom

They are "ten ethical precepts" that allow us to be at peace with Niyamas

1.The Yamas Ahimsa (nonviolence, nonharming), Satya (truthfulness), Asteya (nonstealing), Bramacharya (moderation, restraint, continence), Aparigraha (noncovetousness, non-hoarding).

2. The Niyamas Saucha (cleanliness, purity), Santosha (contentment), Tapas (discipline, heat, spiritual austerities), Svadhyaya (study of the sacred scriptures and of one's self), Ishvara Pranidhana (surrender to God, devotion).

3. Asana Physical postures: forward bending, backward bending, lateral bending, twists, and inversions.

4. Pranayama Releasing and channeling of prana or the body's life force; more commonly, breath control or breathing exercises

5. Pratyahara Senses withdrawal; withdrawal of external stimuli and turning the senses inward.

6. Dharana Concentration (focus on a single mental object): a specific energetic center in the body, an image, a mantra

7. Dhyana Meditation (uninterrupted flow of concentration): the mind has been quieted and produces few or no thoughts.

8. Samadhi Contemplation, absorption, or super-conscious state; also, a state of ecstasy or bliss.

SIMPLE RECOMMENDATIONS FOR APPLYING THE YAMAS AND NIYAMAS ON AND OFF THE MAT

Note: The following suggestions for applying Yogic codes of living as identified in the yamas and niyamas are drawn from various sources as well as the authors' experiences. The Yamas Ahimsa (nonviolence, non-harming): in our Yoga practice, we should seek to be non-harming to ourselves by cultivating awareness and respecting our bodies with its abilities and limitations, rather than forcing our bodies into postures beyond our current abilities and avoiding negative self talk and self-judgment. We also can practice ahimsa toward others by letting go of judgment of and competition with them on our mats. We can practice kindness toward others on and off our mats in a variety of ways, by listening, being present, and practicing compassion and offering assistance when we can. We can treat all beings and all things with care and compassion.

Satya (truthfulness): practicing satya means being honest with ourselves, being truthful in our feelings, thoughts, words, and actions (palkhivala). We also can try to view ourselves objectively, seeing ourselves clearly and honestly, rather than filtering how we see ourselves through the eyes or opinions of others. We can look at the big pictures of our poses or our lives, rather than just the flattering (or unflattering) parts.

Asteya (nonstealing): we can implement asteya in our practice by being courteous to others around us. This can include arriving for class on time, not talking while the teacher is trying to give instruction, following the practice as guided, and not taking away from anyone else's experience. We also can give each posture our full energy, rather than holding back or stealing energy to do the next pose. Asteya can be practiced off our mats by operating out of an abundance-based perception of the universe rather than one grounded in scarcity. It can be practiced in giving credit where credit is due and by living "greener" so that we are not taking away from future generations or the earth. Brahmacharya (restraint, moderation, continence): brahmacharya can be interpreted and practiced in many different ways. We can practice brahmacharya by consciously choosing to use our life force to express our dharma, our true nature and mission or purpose, rather than to dissipate it frivolously in the pursuit of temporary pleasures (palkhivala). We can be aware of under doing and overdoing in our lives and try to keep everything in moderation by listening, feeling, and tuning into our bodies and their needs both on and off our mats. Moderation in consumption, behaviors, and finding a better work-life balance reflect brahmacharya.

Aparigraha (noncovetousness, nonhoarding): this is the opposite of greediness. On our mats, this can mean not being greedy for the teacher's attention and realizing that the rest of the class is deserving of the instructor's adjustments and attention as we are. Aparigraha can be expressed off of our mats in our purchases of material goods. We can buy what we need rather than out of desire for having more and more clothes, a bigger faster car, a nicer house, and so on. We can be more aware of our actual needs and seek to meet them instead of always wanting more.

The Niyamas Saucha (cleanliness, purity): saucha can refer to cleanliness or purity of thought, feeling, or deed. Some simple ways to implement saucha in our Yoga practice is to keep our Yoga clothes, mats, and props (e.g., blocks, straps, blankets) clean and orderly. We also can be aware of what is going on internally in terms of our thoughts and feelings and choose to shift those to purer, healthier, and more positive ways of thinking and feeling about ourselves as we practice

Yoga and about others on and off our mats. We also can change our behavior by avoiding things that make us feel guilty and practicing things that are meaningful and give purpose to our lives.

Samtosha (contentment): in Yoga, samtosha can be practiced by accepting performing an asana to the best of our ability in that moment rather than pursing the perfect posture or most advanced posture possible. This does not mean that we should avoid trying to stretch ourselves and improve our Yoga practice, but that we should focus on accepting what we can do and work at our own levels in ways that are safe and effective for our bodies. Off our mats, we can practice gratitude for who we are, what we have, and the people in our lives. We can learn to be accepting of our abilities, our accomplishments, and our situations and to look for the good in all.

Tapas (discipline, heat, spiritual austerities): tapas can be developed and honed by the regular practice of Yoga. Through a regular Yoga practice, we establish self-discipline and passion that can transfer to other aspects for a healthy lifestyle. Also, in holding poses for longer periods or in attempting poses that are difficult for us physically or otherwise, we develop the ability to be "uncomfortably comfortable" in other situations in our lives as well. We learn perseverance, and we may learn when it does not serve us to continue in a pose or situation when it is no longer beneficial to us.

Svadhyaya (study of the sacred scriptures and of one's self): through the study of sacred texts, we learn to see things in different ways, including how we practice Yoga as a physical discipline, as well as how we are embracing life's journey. On our mats, we can be aware of the physical sensations, thoughts, and feelings or emotions that arise during our Yoga practice. We can learn more about ourselves by cultivating this awareness off our mats, as well. We can learn to discern our motives more clearly and choose different ways of thinking and acting that are more closely aligned with a Yogic lifestyle, that is, that reflect kindness, truthfulness, non-stealing, moderation, non-coveting, purity, contentment, and discipline.

Ishvara pranidhana (surrender to God, devotion): on one level, ishvara pranidhana means allowing ourselves to be receptive and letting go of the things that we cannot control. It is our intentions and our efforts that count. We will learn to do Yoga with both intensity and calmness when we dedicate our practice to the universal life force, of which, we are all a part (palkhivala). On another level, ishvara pranidhana refers to a spiritual faith and relationship built through worship, which may occur in many forms. The usages of sankalpa, or affirmations or even prayers, may be useful in practicing ishvara pranidhana.

The ancient practice of Hatha Yoga is now a mainstream form of exercise whose attractions include multiple health and fitness benefits. Those who wish to deepen or intensify their Hatha Yoga practice beyond asana can accomplish this by adding one or more of the other limbs of Yoga on and off the mat, perhaps starting by incorporating one of the yamas or niyamas. By approaching Yoga from a new perspective, we may experience enhanced health and fitness as well as changes and benefits that extend beyond our mats, taking our practice of Hatha Yoga to more holistic and connected experience.

HATHA YOGA Benefits and Principles for a More Meaningful Practice

Hatha Yoga is classified in the Western world as one type of mind-body exercise (along with Tai Chi, Qi Gong, Pilates, and others) and a type of complementary and alternative medicine that has become a popular and effective form of exercise in healthy, clinical, and athletic populations because of the numerous health and fitness benefits associated with a regular practice. Hatha Yoga involves the practice of physical postures in conjunction with awareness of the breath to help develop mental focus and to connect the mind, body, and spirit. Beyond the physical practice, there are some principles of Yoga that may not be very well known by contemporary fitness enthusiasts that can enhance an existing Yoga practice and offer additional lifestyle benefits.

THE BENEFITS OF A REGULAR YOGA PRACTICE

The regular practice of Hatha Yoga enhances strength, flexibility, and balance and may offer some light to moderate aerobic conditioning as well, depending on the style practiced. Other benefits may be gained from incorporating breath work (pranayama) and meditation as part of, or in addition to, a Hatha Yoga practice. These practices have been shown to provide beneficial effects in numerous health conditions including, but not limited to, cancer, heart disease, asthma, infertility, pregnancy, insomnia, arthritis, fibromyalgia.

HOW SAFE IS YOGA

Yoga is generally considered a safe form of physical activity for healthy people when it's done properly, under the guidance of a qualified instructor. But it's possible to get hurt practicing yoga; just as when participating in other physical activities.

The most common injuries associated with yoga are sprains and strains. Serious injuries are rare. The risk of injury associated with yoga is lower than that for higher impact sports activities. Here are some tips on how to reduce your risk of injury when practicing yoga:

i. Start slowly and learn the basics.

ii. Choose a class that's appropriate for your level. If you're not sure, ask the yoga teacher.

iii. As a beginner, you may want to avoid challenging practices such as headstands, shoulder stands, the lotus position, and forceful breathing. Or, if you do try them, engage in them gently, gradually, and with great care.

iv. Learn about the precautions you need to take if you try a "hot yoga" practice (e.g, Bikram yoga). This form of yoga has special risks related to overheating and dehydration.

v. Don't push yourself beyond your comfort level. If you can't do a pose, ask your teacher to help you modify it. If you feel pain or fatigue, stop and rest.

vi. If you have a health condition, if you're an older person, or if you're pregnant, discuss your needs with your health care providers and your yoga instructor. You may need to modify or avoid some yoga poses and practices. For example, if you have a condition that weakens your bones, you'll need to avoid forceful forms of yoga. If you have glaucoma, you'll need to avoid upside-down positions. It's important to remember that you should use yoga appropriately.

Physical Benefits of Yoga

There are many benefits that are derived from this practice. The positions we have studied so far have the following benefits: train muscles and tendons, helping them to become more **elastic** and **stretchable**. Breathing exercise, on the other hand, is perfect for facilitating muscle stretching. In general, this practice relaxes the body and mind and is an excellent remedy for anxiety, stress and all the deleterious effects of the latter. Let's not forget about posture, joint mobility and blood circulation throughout the body, even for the most peripheral points. And then, although it is not really an aerobic training, it also positively stresses the **cardio-circulatory system**, also improving resistance to efforts. But it doesn't stop there! This oriental discipline, if carried out regularly, can be a solution to different problems that the body often suffers from:

- Insomnia
- Anxiety
- Stress
- Neck Pain
- Back Pain
- Cellulite
- Sciatica

FOR BEGINNERS WHO ARE PREGNANT

Regular physical activity during uncomplicated pregnancies can have many benefits. It can increase or maintain overall fitness, promote healthy weight gain, reduce the risk of gestational diabetes, and improve psychological well-being. Modified yoga is an example of a safe exercise that most pregnant women can do as part of their regular physical activity. It's important, however, that a pregnant woman first be evaluated by her obstetrician or other health care team member to ensure that exercise and modified yoga are safe for her. Certain conditions and complications make exercise unsafe during pregnancy. So it's essential that pregnant women be carefully evaluated before exercise recommendations are made. In addition to yoga's benefits as general physical activity, yoga during pregnancy can help reduce stress, improve flexibility, and encourage focused breathing. Research shows that yoga may also help pregnant women who suffer from anxiety, depression, stress, low-back pain, or sleep disturbances.

Whether a pregnant woman is interested in yoga as part of her regular physical activity or for a specific condition, certain modifications are important to consider.

Yoga classes designed for pregnant women

— Prenatal yoga classes will often teach modified poses that accommodate a pregnant woman's shifting balance and increased joint mobility. Similar modifications can be made by pregnant women who are doing yoga on their own or in other types of yoga classes.

— Certain positions should be avoided, including ones that require standing still or lying on one's back for long periods of time. (These positions may cause a temporary drop in blood pressure.)

— It's important to not become overheated, especially in the first trimester of pregnancy. This is because increasing body core temperature is associated with an increased risk for birth defects. This means that Bikram yoga and hot yoga should be avoided during pregnancy. Exercising and doing yoga at room temperature is safe.

If you have any of the following warning signs when exercising or doing yoga, stop and call your health care provider:

  i. Bleeding from the vagina —Feeling dizzy or faint
  ii. Shortness of breath before starting exercise
  iii. Chest pain
  iv. Headache
  v. Muscle weakness

vi. Calf pain or swelling

vii. Regular, painful contractions of the uterus

viii. Fluid leaking from the vagina.

YOGA FOR HEALTH AND WELL BEING

People who practice yoga believe it has benefits for their general well-being Such as improving sleep and reducing stress. But does it actually do these things? Only a small amount of research has looked at this, and the findings have not been completely consistent. Nevertheless, some preliminary research results suggest that yoga may have several different types of benefits for well-being.

a. Stress Management. Some research indicates that practicing yoga can lead to improvements in physical or psychological aspects of stress.

b. Balance. Several studies that looked at the effect of yoga on balance in healthy people found evidence of improvements.

c. Positive Mental Health. Some but not all studies that looked at the effects of yoga on positive aspects of mental health found evidence of benefits, such as better resilience (mental toughness) or general mental well-being.

d. Health Habits. A survey of young adults showed that practicing yoga regularly was associated with better eating and physical activity habits, such as more servings of fruits and vegetables, fewer servings of sugar-sweetened beverages, and more hours of moderate-to-vigorous activity. But it wasn't clear from this study whether yoga motivates people to practice better health habits or whether people with healthier habits are more likely to do yoga. In another study, however, in which previously inactive people were randomly assigned to participate or not participate in 10 weeks of yoga classes, those who participated in yoga increased their total physical activity

e. Quitting Smoking. Programs that include yoga have been evaluated to see whether they help people quit smoking. In most studies of this type, yoga reduced cigarette cravings and the number of cigarettes smoked. So, yoga may be a helpful addition to smoking cessation programs.

f. Weight Control. In studies of yoga for people who were overweight or obese, practicing yoga has been associated with a reduction in body mass index (BMI; a measure of body fat based on height and weight). An NCCIH-supported comparison of different yoga-based programs for weight control showed that the most helpful programs had longer and more frequent yoga sessions, a longer duration of the overall program, a yoga-based dietary component, a residential component (such as a full weekend to start the program), inclusion of a larger number of elements of yoga, and home practice.

THE ADVANTAGES OF YOGA IN LIFE AS A COUPLE

Moving the deep energy from the bottom up, that is from the earth towards the spiritual, in this way you become aware of your body and feel better about yourself: this is one of the many benefits of yoga, thanks to which you will develop sensitivity and desire. For example, men who practice yoga feel more intense pleasure than a simple ejaculation. They control their breathing better and thanks to the tonic perineum they are able to hold and prolong erection and ejaculation. Also, having a greater awareness of their body and soul, they are more present, they seek intimacy.

Yoga postures that enhance sexuality

There are several exercises that are a great example of the close relationship between yoga and sex, exercises that will help improve your elasticity, endurance and mobility, promote the quality of the sexual act and intensify orgasm. With this in mind we propose two yoga positions for sex, suitable for everyone and to be done daily, even better if you just wake up in the morning.

Udhyana Bandha

While standing, open your legs to hip width. Bend your knees slightly and place your hands on your thighs at knee height. Keep your back straight and shoulders relaxed, head in the extension of the spine. Breathe in and out through your nose and pull your belly in as far as you can. Hold your breath and when you feel the desire to exhale, do it and relax your belly. Wait a few seconds and repeat the sequence 10 times on the first day until you get to a daily practice of 5 minutes.

Ardha Natarajasana

Remaining standing with your legs closed, raise your right leg stretched back, bring your torso and right arm forward while keeping the left along the left thigh. Remain balanced on one leg, with the torso parallel to the floor and with the head always in the extension of the vertebral column. Try to hold the position for 5 seconds on the first day and slowly increase the time until you reach 30 seconds. Remember that breathing is very important to be able to hold the position for a long time. When you exhale remember to bring your belly in to hold the position. At this point, perform the same position with the other leg.

COMPLEMENTARY, INTEGRATIVE, AND ALTERNATIVE HEALTH APPROACHES

If you're using yoga to help manage a health problem, you're using a complementary health approach.

a. A complementary health approach is one that was developed outside of mainstream Western medicine and is used along with conventional medical care.

b. You may hear people talk about integrative health approaches. Integrative health care often brings conventional and complementary approaches together in a coordinated way. It emphasizes a holistic, patient-focused approach to health care and well-being **often including** mental, emotional, functional, spiritual, social, and community aspects and treating the whole person rather than, for example, one organ system. It aims for well-coordinated care between different providers and institutions.

c. Another term you may hear is alternative medicine. Alternative means using an unconventional approach in place of conventional health care. This is actually

Uncommon in the United States. Most people who use health approaches that were developed outside of mainstream Western medicine also see conventional health care providers. The use of complementary and integrative approaches to health and well-being, such as yoga, has increased within health care settings across the United States. Researchers are currently exploring the potential benefits of these approaches in a variety of situations such as pain management for military personnel and veterans, relief of symptoms in cancer patients and survivors, and programs to promote healthy behaviors. If you feel better when you're using a complementary approach for a health problem, you might wonder whether it's OK to decrease or stop your conventional treatment. The answer depends on the health problem, the type of treatment, and your individual situation. It's very important to talk with your health care provider if you're thinking about making any changes in the treatment that's been prescribed or recommended for your health condition.

DISADVANTAGE OF YOGA

Yoga is a way of life for some people. For others, it is a complement to their regular fitness program. And for some, it's a curiosity or something they plan to try. The benefits of an ongoing yoga practice have been described in scientific journals and the number of enthusiasts is growing every day. According to the statistics compiled by "Yoga Journal", there was an increase of 10 million new yoga practitioners from 2001 to 2010. But are there any drawbacks to practicing this system from 5,000 years ago?

Ethics

Finding a teacher who has been certified by a reputable school can be a disadvantage of yoga. There is no law in place that requires certification of a yoga instructor. The closest thing to a government agency is the Yoga Alliance, which is an organization that was put together in 1999 by two groups of volunteers called Unity in Yoga and Ad Hoc Yoga. They have developed a 200 and 500 hour teacher training program that some aspiring teachers feel gives them an edge in the competitive yoga teacher community. But not all people aspiring to become yoga teachers can afford to spend so much time or money on their accreditation and choose to roll out their shingles based on a simple passion for the discipline.

Yoga as a therapy

People seek the benefits of yoga for many different reasons. They may have bodily problems such as overweight or underweight. They may have medical concerns such as multiple sclerosis or chronic back pain. The field of yoga therapy has grown exponentially as more studies target people willing to experiment with healing methods that go beyond traditional medicine. Iyengar yoga, a system that relies on props such as walls and pulleys, was developed by BKS Iyengar in the early 20th century. Iyengar was dealing with his health problems. But finding a yoga therapist who has had the necessary training and is affordable is another disadvantage of yoga.

Capacity

When you think of yoga, you can't help but remember the images of very skinny athletic men and women on magazine covers twisted and folded in shocking poses. Yoga is not exclusively for the slim and fit, but one of the disadvantages of yoga is that not all poses can be practiced by everyone. Men, in particular, don't have the flexibility of women. They make up for it heavily, but yoga is about to push your limits, and injuries can happen when men try too hard.

CONCLUSION

Yoga is a systematic practice of physical exercise, breath control, relaxation, diet control, and positive thinking and meditation aimed at developing harmony in the body, mind, and environment. Most people are familiar with the physical poses or yoga positions but don't know that yoga involves so much more. A mind and body practice with a 5,000-year history in ancient Indian philosophy. Various styles of yoga combine physical postures, breathing techniques, and meditation or relaxation. There are several different types of yoga and many disciplines within the practice.

The practice enhances resilience and improves mind-body awareness, which can help people adjust their behaviors based on these feelings they. Practicing Restorative yoga can have enormous benefits for healing, both body and mind but when the pace of life is fast, we may find our minds and bodies speed up to match it. Our minds start to race, we can feel overwhelmed, and drained. If we are also drawn to a strong, dynamic yoga practice or other high intensity exercise, then we may get over stimulated. Our nervous systems then take a beating. Making sure we take some time out to practice

Restorative yoga even once a week can help to balance our busy lifestyles and has an enormous capacity to heal stress-related physical and emotional issues. Despite a growing body of clinical research studies and some systematic reviews on the therapeutic effects of yoga, there is still a lack of solid evidence regarding its clinical relevance for many symptoms and medical conditions. For many specific indications and conditions, there is inconsistent evidence with several studies reporting positive effects of the yoga interventions, but other studies are less conclusive. In some instances, these discrepancies may result from differences between the study populations (e.g, age, gender, and health status), the details of the yoga interventions, and follow-up rates. Practicing yoga helps provide a foundation and tools to building good habits, such as discipline, self-inquiry, and non-attachment. This exercise is also a pathway. In Restorative yoga class we use props like bolsters, blankets and blocks to completely support the body in poses and we stay there for up to 10 minutes per pose. There is no muscular effort involved so restorative yoga can also be helpful to try if you are chronically ill or recovering from injury.